*River scene in the 1930s. A sailing barge taking in sail.*

# SAILING BARGES

## Martin Hazell

# A Shire book

# CONTENTS

British Library Cataloguing in Publication Data: Hazell, Martin. Sailing Barges. – 3rd ed. – (A Shire album; 13) 1. Sailing barges – England – History I. Title 387.2'2'0942. ISBN 0 7478 0492 3.

Cover: *The sailing barge 'Kitty'. The barge bowsprit is raised. The jib is backing and the barge is about to change course. Also note the tear appearing in the topsail.*

ACKNOWLEDGEMENTS
The author wishes to thank the following people and organisations for help received: the late Harold Farrington-House and numerous bargemen; Peter Ferguson, Alan Cordell and members of the Society for Spritsail Barge Research and the Thames Barge Sailing Club.
Illustrations are acknowledged as follows: A. Cordell Collection, pages 7 (top), 11, 23 (both), 24 (both), 25 (left), 27; P. Ferguson Collection, page 10 (centre); Science Museum, London, Crown copyright, pages 5, 6 (top right), 26 (bottom); Photograph, Science Museum, London, pages 3, 4 (both), 6 (top left), 9; Society for Spritsail Barge Research – Dowsett Collection, pages 7 (bottom); 8 (top), 10 (top), 22; author's collection, pages 1, 6 (bottom), 8 (bottom), 10 (bottom), 12 (all), 13 (all), 14 (both), 15 (all), 18 (bottom), 19, 20 (both), 21, 25 (right), 26 (top), 30, and front cover; Thames Barge Sailing Club (copyright R. S. Wood), pages 28-9. The sailing barge on pages 16-17 and the map on page 18 were drawn by Peter Ferguson.

*Published in 2001 by Shire Publications Ltd, Cromwell House, Church Street, Princes Risborough, Buckinghamshire HP27 9AA, UK. (Website: www.shirebooks.co.uk)*
*Copyright © 1976, 1982 and 2001 by Martin Hazell. First published 1976. Second edition 1982; reprinted 1986 and 1990. Third edition 2001. Shire Album 13. ISBN 0 7478 0492 3.*
*Martin Hazell is hereby identified as the author of this work in accordance with Section 77 of the Copyright, Designs and Patents Act 1988.*

Printed in Great Britain by CIT Printing Services Ltd, Press Buildings, Merlins Bridge, Haverfordwest, Pembrokeshire SA61 1XF.

*A group of cutter-rigged barges which have no sprit, but instead the mainsail is attached to a boom and to hoops which are hauled up the mast (from an etching made by E. W. Cooke in 1828).*

# HISTORY OF THE SAILING BARGE

Barges are flat-bottomed freight carriers. The canal barges of old were usually hauled by horses or teams of men; sometimes they set sails when there were favourable winds. Perhaps the finest development of the barge form, however, is the river Thames spritsail sailing barge.

Many people visiting the south-east coast of England may well have seen a sailing barge, for these are home waters for this relic from the age of sail. No other sailing vessel in Britain survived for so long in trade. Although the maid of all work, the sailing barge was not usually slow or ugly. This vessel was the ultimate development of the small sailing trader. She was cheap to build and run, for the wind was free and the wages of the crew low, and before the advent of the motor lorry speed of delivery was not all-important and the sailing barge held her own as an efficient and economic form of transport. Some vessels were built to beautiful lines and had a fine turn of speed. It is little wonder that marine artists of the calibre of William L. Wyllie have frequently depicted these 'sailormen' of the London river, as they were called.

The Thames sailing barge has a number of special features. Like all barges it has a flat-bottomed hull enabling the vessel to sit on the bed of shallow rivers and creeks when the tide recedes (the east coast of England is mainly flat). Like the Dutch barge, the sailing barge has a pair of leeboards. These are raised and lowered depending which point of sailing the vessel is on. A sailing barge draws very little water – only a matter of a few feet – and to make good sailing headway a leeboard can be lowered to add depth underneath the keel in order that the barge grips the water better and does not drift, or make leeway, sideways. Another feature of the Thames sailing barge is the sprit (hence the full name spritsail sailing barge). This is a great spar crossing

3

Above: *Four early 'stumpy' barges. Note crew members wearing protective headwear for possible handling of cargoes of refuse or mud.*

Left: *A laden barge off Northfleet, Kent, in 1829. Square topsails died out after 1870. In this picture the artist seems to have put the sprit on the wrong side of the mainsail. Both pictures are from etchings by E. W. Cooke, made in 1828 and 1829.*

and supporting the mainsail diagonally from the base of the mast to the top or 'peak' of the sail. In order to pass under the numerous bridges spanning the rivers the mainmast rests in a mastcase and can be lowered. (See the diagram on pages 16–17 for details of parts of the modern sailing barge.)

The final sailing barge form developed slowly from the small box-like craft and one-masted passenger and cargo-carrying hoy of the eighteenth century. The 'dumb' (towed) lighters which were used on the river Thames are quite close in hull shape to those vessels of the eighteenth century. By the closing years of the eighteenth century miniature versions of the hoys, or one-masted coasting vessels, appeared, fitted out

*Model of a seventeenth-century Dutch barge. This traditional vessel still survives and is similar to the Thames barge in that it has leeboards and a flat-bottomed hull.*

with leeboards and sometimes setting a squaresail, but increasingly spritsail rigged. This spritsail rig is not unique and was used in Holland in the Middle Ages, and some of the early Thames sailing vessels had this rig by the seventeenth century. The barges of the early 1800s with square overhanging ends ('swim heads') or round bows were entirely open. They were not coastal craft yet and were quite small, being only from about 20 to 25 tons. As the vessels became bigger, an extra sail was required to assist handling, and about the year 1800 the mizzen mast and sail were added. At first this mast was fixed to the rudder post. By 1810 decks were being fitted and hatch covers were made to cover the one large hold. The rounded bow began to supersede the

Above left: *Contemporary print of a Thames barge in 1809, clearly showing the primitive steering arrangement, massive sprit and leeboard.*

Above right: *Model of a topsail barge of the second quarter of the nineteenth century. Although decked and having a bowsprit, this barge still has the mizzenmast attached to the rudder head (top) and she is steered by a tiller.*

Left: *The 'stumpy' river barge 'Lady of the Lee', re-rigged and sailing again in 1979 for the first time since she was sold out of trade after the Second World War. Built in 1931 for the government explosives trade between Waltham Abbey and Woolwich Arsenal, she is the only surviving example of a small narrow river barge steered by a tiller. She now supports a topsail and wheel steering.*

swim head from about 1840, and the transom or square stern came in after 1860. The wheel for steering was not introduced until about 1880. Before this the tiller had to be pushed over by hand to bring the vessel about. When changing course the addition of a small mizzensail attached to the rudder helped to push the vessel round.

Most nineteenth-century barges had only three sails – the foresail, the mainsail or spritsail, and the mizzensail. Soon bigger barges were setting topsails from a topmast. This was usual after 1890. The mainsail's name derives from the sprit, usually made out of Oregon or pitch pine, which is attached to the base of the mainmast on the starboard (right) side. The sprit extends up and out to the peak (top) of the mainsail, and thus there is no main boom spar to hinder loading and unloading of cargo. 'Stumpy' barges were smaller vessels without topsails, and they survived well into the twentieth century.

*The launching of the 'Olive May', built by Wills & Packham Ltd at Crown Quay, Sittingbourne, in 1920. She was the only sailing barge built with a motor.*

*A sailing barge that has just shot Rochester bridge in Kent. The mainmast, secured at deck level into a three-sided mastcase, is lowered to the deck by letting out the stayfall slowly. See the wire rope above the men. The weight is taken on the windlass. When the barge has been carried by its momentum under the bridge, the mast is raised again. The shooting of a bridge required great skill but enabled barges to reach far inland. For this task a third hand or 'huffler' was hired. Sailing barges never shoot bridges these days as it is a dangerous task in a crowded waterway.*

7

*A barge, with gear lowered, being rowed underneath Blackfriars Bridge, London, about 1900. The large oars, about 20 feet (6 metres) in length, are called sweeps.*

By 1900 larger coasting barges of over 100 tons with bowsprits were being built frequently. Further sails could be set from this extra spar, extending forward from the bow of the barge. Although essentially river and coasting vessels, barges of the larger sort often ventured across the English Channel. Wooden, and latterly steel-hulled, sailing barges were built up to 1931, but by then increasingly these vessels were being

*Humber sloops c.1930. They had only one mast and a main boom extending over the hatch cover, instead of the sprit. The leeboard is clearly seen. Sloops carried two crew and often traded as far south as Suffolk. This type is now extinct.*

*Model of a Humber or Yorkshire keel. These vessels, which died out after the Second World War, were inland waterways craft.*

cut down and converted to full, or auxiliary, motor power.

The river and coastal barge trade probably reached a peak around 1914 when well over two thousand sailing barges were employed carrying cargoes of all varieties. Evolution, based upon economic efficiency, produced the type of barge still seen today, which is easy to sail – needing only two men – and an object of some grace and beauty.

The numbers of barges registered in various years is approximately as follows (based upon the Mercantile Navy List and Maritime Directory: probably not all of the river-registered barges were included in this directory): 1885, 2019 vessels; 1907, 2090; 1918, 1650; 1930, 1100; 1939, 600; 1950, 181 (mainly auxiliary and motor-powered); 1966, 1 vessel under sail, plus 70 motor barges; in the early 1980s about 50 barges, either rigged or semi-rigged or being rigged as barge yachts. In 2000 the number of barge yachts in existence was still about 50.

Left: *Sailing barges and a lighter in Ipswich docks (date unknown). This clearly shows the variation in hull shape of these vessels.*

Right: *Model of a coasting barge showing the barge boat on the davits (usually on the starboard or right-hand side) and the wheelhouse. River barges do not have a wheelhouse.*

*'Stumpy' river barges at Ware on the river Lea, Hertfordshire, in the early years of the twentieth century. These barges do not set topsails and have no topmasts. River barges were built unusually narrow in order to fit into river locks and, in earlier times, squaresails would have been set. Latterly horses, and even special tractors, were used for barge towing on the Lea.*

10

*The sailing barge 'Mercy' at Milton Creek, 1899, showing the position of the leeboard. Leeboards are usually made of oak planks 12–15 inches (30–38 cm) wide and 3 inches (7.6 cm) thick strapped together with iron bands, and about 17 feet (5.2 metres) long. The widest part of the leeboard is usually equal to the depth of the barge's side.*

# ANATOMY OF THE SAILING BARGE

Sir Alan Herbert wrote of the sailing barge in *The Singing Swan*, 'Everything about her was practical before it was beautiful and was beautiful because it was right.' Very few sailing barges indeed were built to plans, and very few, if any, were alike. In East Anglia the Cann-built barges, heavy lined to withstand coastal passages, but fast and graceful, were different in shape from the Howard-built Maldon barges of Essex, which were shallower and broader. A glance at the sterns of surviving barges will reveal the difference in shape and curve of so many of these vessels.

Sailing barges ranged generally from about 40 to 120 tons although a few larger metal-hulled vessels (the 'ironpots') were constructed. Barges were rarely over 100 feet (30 metres) long or over 20 feet (6 metres) wide at their extreme breadth. The depth of a sailing barge could range from about 5 to 8 feet (1.5 to 2.4 metres) from keel to deck level. Some barges such as the *Lady of the Lea* were built especially narrow in order to be able to navigate certain rivers and canals.

Wooden barge-building and sailmaking were craftsmen's jobs. Using simple tools, like the auger (hand drill) and adze (curved axe) and by steaming planks in steamchests to enable them to be curved and pliable, the shipwright built up a wooden vessel by rule of thumb from the bottom, or keel, up. The art of wooden barge-building may now be lost (the last wooden barge was constructed in 1931) but there are still a few hand sailmakers surviving.

The barge illustrating pages 12–15 is the Thames Barge Sailing Club vessel *Pudge* – one of the last to be built. She is wooden-hulled, of 67 tons, was launched in 1922 and is a Dunkirk veteran.

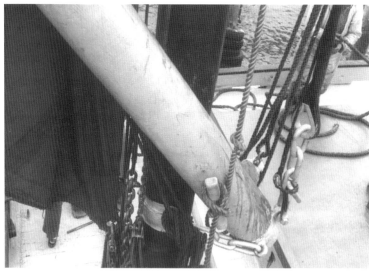

*A view of the great sprit, showing how it is connected to the mainmast.*

Below left: *The view aft showing the deck covers of the large main hold, the main horse, and the leeboard winches which are just behind the horse.*

Below right: *The main horse of a barge. The foot of the mainsail is attached to a block which in turn hooks on to an iron ring with an eye (the traveller) situated on the horse. This enables the mainsail to be set for various points of sailing, the sail being guided over the deck in a controlled way. The foresail is also controlled by a horse, but in a slightly different way.*

Above: *Working the leeboard winch. The heavy wooden leeboard has the narrow end bolted to a chain that extends across the foredeck (see bottom picture on the following page – chain by crewman's feet). The end which is lowered into the water is held by a chain and wire which is wound on to the winch. In this picture the leeboard is being lowered carefully, the winch handle controlling the speed at which the wire is being played out.*

Right: *A barge windlass. On the small drum above the main barrel is a long, light and very strong wire line which can be run out in a boat, secured and then wound in. In this way a barge can be hauled on to a buoy or across a dock.*

Below: *Taking up the anchor on the windlass. A barge may carry up to sixty fathoms of chain.*

13

Above: *Two members of a charter barge crew brailing in the great mainsail. Also note that the foresail has been half run down on the forestay.*

Left: *The view forward. The mainsail is gathered in on to the mast by the hauling in of three brails which pass round the sail – the 'lowers' and 'middles' of rope, the main brail of wire. Here the crewman with the aid of a winch is tightening in the main brail.*

Left: *The foresheetman. Since this sail is important in helping to drive a barge round, it is controlled by having a bowline hooked through a metal eye which is fixed near to the foot of the sail. The bowline can be held or tied to the mainmast rigging.*

Below left: *The view from deck level, showing the barge's mainmast and topmast, with foresail, mainsail and topsail.*

Below right: *The sailing barge, being shaped like a flat box, has four or six pump wells, so that, whichever way the vessel tilts, water must run into one of the corners. The pump handle is hinged to a metal upright which slots into a hole adjacent to the well. The suction pad and rod fix on to the pump handle by means of a hook. A bucket of water is poured into the well, and steady pumping gives suction and thus bilge water is raised. Note the main horse and foot of the mainsail attached by means of the block and traveller.*

drawn by
PETER FERGUSON.

KEY :

| | | | |
|---|---|---|---|
| 1. | Staysail/Jib Topsail | 29. | Mizzen shrouds |
| 2. | Jib | 30. | Mizzen sheet |
| 3. | Foresail | 31. | Main sheet |
| 4. | Topsail | 32. | Main brail |
| 5. | Mainsail | 33. | Davits |
| 6. | Mizzen | 34. | Cabin scuttle hatch |
| 7. | Bowsprit | 35. | Cabin skylight |
| 8. | Mainmast | 36. | Wheel |
| 9. | Top mast | 37. | Main horse |
| 10. | Sprit | 38. | Main hatch |
| 11. | Mizzen mast | 39. | Fore horse |
| 12. | Mizzen sprit | 40. | Fore hatch |
| 13. | Mizzen boom | 41. | Foc'sle hatch |
| 14. | Cross trees | 42. | Windlass |
| 15. | Bob. | 43. | Anchor |
| 16. | Head stick | 44. | Bow badge |
| 17. | Starboard shrouds | 45. | Stem |
| 18. | Main runners | 46. | Rails |
| 19. | Fore stay | 47. | Covering board |
| 20. | Stayfall tackle | 48. | Wale |
| 21. | Standing backstays | 49. | Chine |
| 22. | Running backstays | 50. | Run |
| 23. | Topmast stay | 51. | Coamings |
| 24. | Jib stay | 52. | Head ledge |
| 25. | Bob stay | 53. | Rigging chock |
| 26. | Bowsprit shrouds | 54. | Lee board |
| 27. | Yard tackle | 55. | Rudder |
| 28. | Wang | 56. | Quarter board |

# Coastal Sailing Barge circa 1900

# The Barge Coast

drawn by
PETER FERGUSON

*The Butt and Oyster Inn at Pin Mill, the sailing barge centre on the river Orwell, where a variety of barges, rigged, unrigged and hulks, are to be seen all the year round. Photographed in the 1970s, the scene is much the same today.*

18

*Cook's boat shed and barge repair yard at Maldon in 1971, with the church, the Jolly Sailor pub and Hythe Quay in the background. The Thames Barge Sailing Club barge 'Westmoreland' is alongside awaiting repairs. Maldon was and still is an important barge centre and many barges can sometimes be seen alongside the quay. Maldon is a charter barge centre and finishing point for the modern Blackwater sailing-barge match. There has been little change in this view since the photograph was taken.*

# THE BARGE COAST

The spritsail sailing barge was mainly built on, and traded from, the south-east coast of England, although some were built further afield. The main barge-building centres were at Harwich and Ipswich, Maldon on the river Blackwater, various places along the river Thames, the river Medway, and in Kentish creeks as far as Whitstable.

Year by year barge remains are further broken up or burnt, but, given a good map, a stout pair of boots and perhaps even planking to bridge the muddy wastes, it is surprising what can be found. Remains in Norfolk and in the river Deben are few and difficult to reach while many of the remains in the river Orwell and Stour areas are barely visible. However, wrecks and houseboats, as well as rigged barges, are to be found at Pin Mill on the Orwell, around the Maldon area and in Heybridge Creek on the Blackwater. Many Thames-side creeks have remains, and in Kent the backwaters of the Medway and the Isle of Thanet and Swale area were, in places, thick with aged or decaying hulks. Whitewall Creek, near Rochester, was the resting ground of at least thirty sailing barges. Barge hulks and wrecks have been found as far afield as the south coasts of Devon and Cornwall.

Many barges have converted into fine houseboats. The *Favorite*, built in 1803, rebuilt in 1898 and trading as late as 1929, finally became a houseboat and was afloat in 1940. The upper reaches of the Thames and Medway will reveal a number of floating homes converted from former trading sailing barges.

*A barge hulk in Queenborough Creek, Isle of Sheppey, in 1975. The Society for Barge Research locates and records surviving hulks and sometimes salvages objects such as barge wheels, name badges and, in this case, decorated bow badges. Each barge-builder had his own style of design and colouring for scrollwork and name badges.*

*Charter barges at Hythe Quay, Maldon, on the river Blackwater. Note the barge hulk on the saltings in the distance. The Thames Barge Sailing Club vessels are based here and during the winter members carry out maintenance on the craft.*

*Collecting mud. Barges, being flat-bottomed craft, were ideal for collecting mud and sand for use in cement and brick making. The vessel would drop anchor and wait for the tide to fall. When dry, the skipper and mate, sometimes joined by a sandheaver, would load the barge hold, using spades throwing up about 28 pounds (13 kg). It could take seven or eight hours of back-breaking work for four men to fill a hold. This work was mainly done in winter when freights might be fewer. Before the Second World War barges used to carry away large quantities of sand from Leigh 'sandhill', off Southend.*

# CARGOES

Sailing barges were designed primarily for moving bulk cargoes from shallow soft-bedded rivers and other confined waters. Indeed, the bargemen would say their craft could go anywhere after a heavy dew and turn to windward up a drainpipe! Coasting barges traded across the North Sea, and between 1926 and 1933 four large schooner barges even sailed to British Guiana in South America. The smaller river barges pushed their noses as far inland as Reading and Hertford, Colchester and Aylesford (Kent). Some barges, specially built, negotiated the Regent's Canal in London, and, before modern dock facilities and containerisation, sailing barges were used to unload large cargo vessels in the Thames.

The cargoes carried were enormously varied. East Anglian farmers would load grain and hay (for London's cab horses) and the vessels would often return with horse manure for the farms. In the early days of the nineteenth century, towns such as Maldon and Woodbridge, isolated from the main centres, imported many of their necessities up the rivers in the sailing barges. In the later nineteenth century a great trade in bricks and cement started as London rapidly expanded, but this traffic fell away with the advent of motorised transport after 1918. Kentish barges carried

21

*A 'stack' barge loading hay for London's horses (date unknown). When sailing, the mate had to sit on top of the stack of hay to guide the skipper at the tiller.*

building materials to the ever growing London and returned with either coke for the brick-making ovens or city refuse for dumping. In winter, barges often loaded sand and mud from the coastal areas for use in the making of bricks. From Hertfordshire came market-garden produce and malt, while timber was loaded on to barges at Ipswich and London docks for shipment to the various small towns along the east-coast rivers. The list is endless. One of the last wooden sailing barges built was the *Lady of the Lea* in 1931 for the War Department for service at Waltham Abbey and Woolwich Arsenal.

Until the end of the sailing-barge era, barges often served in specific trades. Below is an extract from the cargo book of the barge *Sidwell*, owned by a brick-manufacturing firm at Sittingbourne, Kent.

| Date loaded (1923) | Cargo | Where loaded | Shipper | Where discharged | Consignee | Date discharged (1923) |
|---|---|---|---|---|---|---|
| 3rd January | 100 yards flint | Murston | Smeed Dean | Barking | East Ham Council | 6th-8th January |
| 9th January | 71 tons coke | Bromley gasworks | Gas Council | Murston | Smeed Dean | 15th January |
| 16th January | 10,000 bricks 78 tons cement | Murston | Smeed Dean | Mendip Wharf Battersea | Dawson | 19th January |
| 22nd-23rd January | Refuse | Battersea | Borough Council | Murston | Smeed Dean | 25th January |
| 26th January | 105 tons cement | Murston | Smeed Dean | Southend | Lamb | 1st February |
| 6th February | 71 tons coke | Bromley | Gas Council | Murston | Smeed Dean | 12th February |
| 13th February | 45,000 bricks | Murston | Smeed Dean | Twickenham | Dawson | 19th February |

*The 'Sidwell', a typical working barge, seen here off Leigh in 1936. She was built in 1877 and ended her life as a munitions hulk during the Second World War. Many barges when fully loaded had a freeboard from the water of only a few inches.*

*Barges, with topmasts lowered, at Bow Creek before the Second World War. The barge 'Alice Laws', on the right of the picture, has unloaded, but the 'John Byford' (centre) still awaits unloading as she sits lower in the water because of the weight of the cargo.*

*Adelaide Dock, Murston, by Milton Creek, Kent, about 1930. Brickfields can be seen in the background.*

*The barge 'Histed' being loaded with bricks at Adelaide Dock about 1930. Note the barge main hold with the hatch covers stacked in front of the wheel. An average-sized barge could carry forty thousand bricks.*

# BARGE CREWS

The average sailing barge carried only a master and a mate, although some large coasting vessels had a third hand. In some trades loading and unloading were done by the crew. Most sailing barges were owned by industrial firms or farmers, although there were quite a few cases of skipper owners in the nineteenth century in particular. Crews' wages were low; often 50 per cent of freight money earned went to the owner while the other 50 per cent was divided – usually in a ratio of two to one – between the skipper and mate. Some owners never paid crews when the vessels were windbound or unable to find cargoes. The 'starvation buoys' at Woolwich were infamous to crews in the 1930s as the point on the river Thames where out-of-work barges lay.

In the olden days barge mates were mere lads direct from school. Good mates might expect to be given a barge by the time they were twenty-one. Some skipper owners even lived on board the vessels with their families, and the barge cat or dog was, and indeed still is, quite common.

In the later barge races it was not uncommon for a race crew – of up to six – all to be experienced barge masters. Some skippers were famous for the number of cups and winner's pennants that they obtained in the races. The Horlock family of Mistley between them must have gained over a hundred honours. Many of the early yacht-barge skippers were men who were famous racing masters over a quarter of a century before. With a lifetime's experience of the tidal shoal waters of the south-east coast, and a professional's cunning, a seventy- or eighty-year-old skipper could equal any youngster in races, as results showed. Present-day yacht-barge skippers learnt their skills as youngsters who assisted the old professionals in the 1960s and 1970s.

Above left: *Mrs Ada Fletcher of Sittingbourne, when aged ninety. She spent seven years as mate to her husband, helping to ship cement to such places as Dartford, Limehouse and Kingston.*

Above right: *The late Harold Farrington-House, regular skipper for the Thames Barge Sailing Club in the 1960s, on board the club barge 'Pudge' in 1975.*

*A barge mate stowing in the topsail, which has been lowered by lashing it to the standard rigging of the great mainmast.*

*Model of a Norfolk wherry similar to the 'Albion', the vessel restored by the Wherry Society.*

*Often barges carried advertisements on their sails. Here the little barge 'Westmoreland', belonging to Eastwoods, the brickmakers and barge-owners, is seen in the 1961 Medway barge match. She was later presented to the Thames Barge Sailing Club and is now being rebuilt at Faversham, Kent, after breaking her back. The 'Westmoreland' is an example of the smaller river staysail barges – that is, a barge without a bowsprit extending forward over the stem of the vessel on to which the jib sail is attached.*

# BARGE RACES

Bargemen were inveterate racers, probably because in some barge fleets the cargo was given to the first barge to arrive. It was William Henry Dodd who in the 1860s sponsored sailing-barge matches in an attempt to encourage better design and building of barges, and fine crews. Dodd, known as the 'golden dustman', had made his fortune from the carting away of London rubbish in sailing barges and considered the coasting and barging trade the 'true school for the Navy'. He endowed the sailing-barge matches through a bequest of £5000 to the Fishmongers' Company.

The Thames and Medway races were the major events and in due course firms often had vessels specially built or equipped for racing. To win the champion's pennant meant more than honour and some money for the winning owner and crew – it often brought increased freight business.

The final races for working craft were held in 1963 – one hundred years after the first river Thames sailing-barge match. However, there have since been barge matches for non-trading sailing barges, and many of these vessels are now entering racing again after an absence of many years. Each year there are six or more barge matches (weather permitting), starting from places such as Southend, Chatham, Pin Mill on the river Orwell, the river Blackwater and the Kentish Swale.

It is now quite common for up to ten converted yacht barges to enter the barge matches, and, as in previous years, the races represent the highlight of the 'sailor-man's' year. Most converted barges have their main holds adapted to take up to twelve passengers and the majority of the vessels taking part in the present-day races can be chartered. Following craft are often available for spectators wishing to view the barge matches, which sometimes entail a sail of up to eight hours for race crews. Dates of sailing-barge matches do vary from year to year but it is usual for at least one race to take place on a bank holiday Saturday or Monday. Programmes can usually be bought, and some of the races finish up with a supper for competitors in the evening, at which cups are presented, stories told and races relived. The national and local press generally carry details of the barge races.

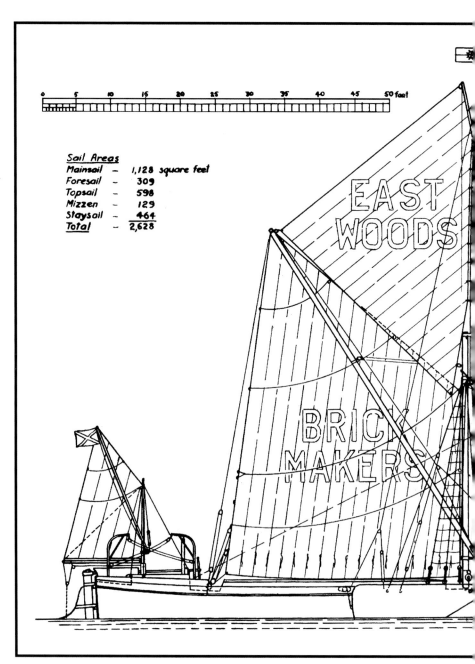

**Sail Areas**

| | | |
|---|---|---|
| Mainsail | – | 1,128 square feet |
| Foresail | – | 309 |
| Topsail | – | 598 |
| Mizzen | – | 129 |
| Staysail | – | 464 |
| Total | – | 2,628 |

*Drawing of the small sailing barge 'Westmoreland', formerly owned by Eastwoods, the brickmakers, but later presented to the Thames Barge Sailing Club.*

# WESTMORELAND

*Thames Barge Sailing Club* © *1969* *R.Wood*

Eastwoods Ltd. **bob**

18 ins

Blue   White   Red

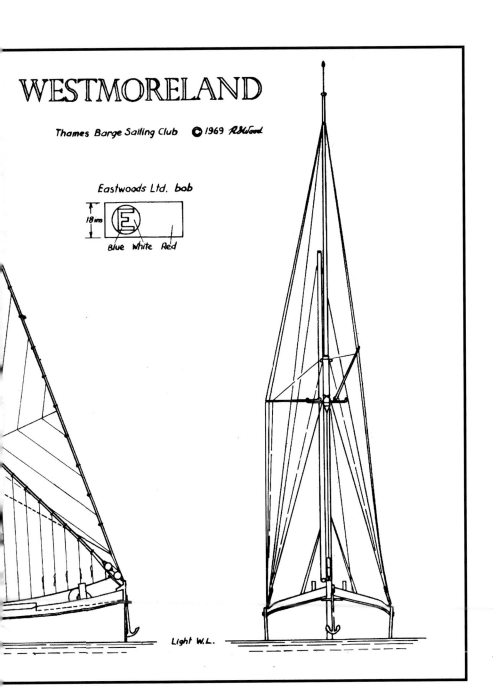

Light W.L.

# PRESENT AND FUTURE

Many sailing barges are today owned by individuals or companies who equip them for charter work. No vessels sail under trade nowadays. The *May*, however, built in 1891 and one of the oldest survivors, in 1972 loaded 50 tons of Portland stone and delivered it to St Paul's Cathedral to be used in the restoration of the building. The last barge to trade under sail was Bob Roberts's *Cambria*. She finally ceased work in 1970 and was acquired by the Maritime Trust for display as a museum ship. She is now undergoing major works at the Dolphin Trust barge yard at Sittingbourne, Kent.

Two large coastal barges, *Thalatta* and *Xylonite*, are used as training vessels for educational purposes. The Thames Barge Sailing Club, founded in 1948, owns the *Pudge* and *Centaur* and uses these vessels for weekend sailing for members and also for charter work.

In any one year there may be thirty or more rigged sailing barges cruising Britain's rivers and coastal waters. Most vessels now have auxiliary power, and all are subject to the strictest Board of Trade scrutiny. Thames sailing barges are even to be seen at European maritime regattas and heritage events. Most of the coastline of the British Isles has been visited by barges advertising a brand of whisky. This idea of barge advertising is not new, for in olden days these vessels would often carry advertisements on their sails.

The Thames sailing barge will survive for many years to come. Although no cargo-

*A forest of masts. Barges moored off Butler's Wharf, Pool of London, after the Port of London Clipper Regatta sailing-barge match in August 1975. Eventually over twenty barges were moored in the Pool, a sight not seen for many years.*

30

carrying craft have been built since the 1930s, if well maintained they can last for well over a hundred years. Half the current sailing barges in commission have steel hulls and these may well outlast their wooden cousins. The cost of maintaining a barge and the difficulty of obtaining timber and sailing gear are becoming a problem as costs rise and skilled traditional shipwrights are at a premium. However, it is not beyond possibility that in the future new sailing barges will be built in some numbers as the maritime heritage industry expands. A new barge has already been built of steel in Canada, and another is under construction in England.

The large coaster *Cambria*, when built in 1906, cost £1895. During the depression years of the 1930s sailing barges, including all gear, could be bought for as little as £200. In the early 1990s an old sailing barge could cost a basic £50,000, and when fully restored could command a six-figure sum. At Maldon the barge yards are busy and at the Dolphin Yard in Sittingbourne, Kent, owners carry out their own repair and refitting work.

The Society for Sailing Barge Research, founded in 1963, has published research, lists current vessels and their history and has compiled a register of barge wrecks and remains.

Further afield, on the Norfolk Broads, the wherry *Albion* has been restored and used for cruising by members of the Wherry Society. These single-masted, flat-bottomed craft, like the Humber and Tyne keels, were similar to the small river sailing barges of the Thames in that they all traded along the shallow rivers of the English east coast.

On the river Humber the Keel and Sloop Preservation Society was founded in 1970 and in 1974, with aid from the Science Museum and the Maritime Trust, it bought and re-rigged the keel *Comrade*. The steel sloop *Amy Howson* was next restored into sailing condition.

The flat-bottomed barge form of the river Severn, the trow, has made a comeback in recent times with the rebuilding of the *Spry* by the Upper Severn Navigation Trust. In north Devon the local gravel barge type survived in the form of the *Advance*. The river Tamar barge *Shamrock* has been restored and is moored at Cotehele Quay, Cornwall, where there is also a museum including details of the Tamar barge family.

However, the only barge form to survive in any great numbers and to remain in sailing order to a great extent is the river Thames spritsail barge. With the rise of the maritime heritage movement in the last two decades of the twentieth century east coast barges have appeared to an even wider audience. For example, *Kitty*, once out of Maldon in Essex, and which the author first sailed on in 1966, is now based on the Solent and in 2000 travelled to the Festival of the Sea in Brest, France. The distinctive red-ochred sails and massive sprits and leeboards of the Thames sailing barges will be seen for many years to come, serving out their time as pleasure and yacht barges and evoking memories of a now lost era, the age of working sail. They are a worthy memorial to the craftsmen and seamen who, with great skill, built them and sailed them – the last of the British sailormen.

# FURTHER READING

The following books relate to the river Thames spritsail sailing barge and may be available by post from the sales officer of the Thames Barge Sailing Club.

Bagshaw, A. and C. (edited by R. Walsh). *Coasting Sailorman*. Chaffcutter Books, 1998.
Carr, F.G.G. *Sailing Barges*. T. Dalton, revised edition 1989. Definitive work.
Durham, R. *The Last Sailorman*. T. Dalton, 1989.
Horlock, A.H. and R.J. *Mistleyman's Log*. Fisher Nautical, 1977.
Roberts, A.W. *Breeze for a Bargeman*. T. Dalton, 1981.
Roberts, A.W. *Coasting Bargemaster*. T. Dalton, 1983.
Roberts. A.W. *Last of the Sailormen*. Reprinted by Seafarer Books, 1986.

The following book is now out of print but is a collectors' item:
March, E.J. *Spritsail Barges of the Thames and Medway*. David & Charles, 1981.

Other titles available from the Thames Barge Sailing Club which relate to practical sailing skills and more recent times are:

Beckett, R. *The Thames Sailing Barge – A Guide*. 1994.
Hearn, P. *Sailing a Thames Barge – Sail by Sail*. 1995.
Thames Barge Sailing Club. *Centaur, Commemoration of a Century*. 1995.
Thames Barge Sailing Club. *The Golden Chaffcutter – A History of the TBSC*. 1998.

There have been many regional studies. For East Anglia see books by Benham, Simper and Finch; for Kent see works by Perks, Sattin and Willmott. Nautical Pictorial have produced three volumes of postcards. Further afield, local barge forms have been recorded by Grant and Hughes (north Devon), D. Wood (river Lea powder barges of Hertfordshire) and Captain F. Schofield's *Humber Keels and Keelmen* (T. Dalton, 1988) while Clark's *Black Sailed Traders* deals with keels and wherries of Norfolk and Suffolk. The National Maritime Museum has published *The Restoration of the Tamar Barge Shamrock, 1974–9*.
    The development of private yacht barges is illustrated by the works of A. S. Bennett and Peggy Larkin. An artist who painted barges was William L. Wyllie (1851–1931) and his *London to the Nore* (Black & Company, 1904) may still be found.
    Recordings of barge songs and stories, by Bob Roberts, may be obtained from specialist folk-music shops.

# PLACES TO VISIT

*Cotehele Quay,* St Dominick, Saltash, Cornwall PL12 6TA. Telephone: 01579 350830. The restored Tamar barge *Shamrock* is on display.
*Dolphin Sailing Barge Museum,* Crown Quay Lane, Sittingbourne, Kent ME10 3SN. Telephone: 01795 424132. A former bargeyard open on Sundays and bank holidays in the summer, where ongoing barge repairs are carried out. The *Cambria*, the last barge to sail in trade, is in dock under repairs (2001).
*Guildhall Museum,* High Street, Rochester, Kent ME1 1PY. Telephone: 01634 848717.

Centres of modern east coast barging are Maldon in Essex, which is the home base of many charter barges and contains working repair yards, Faversham and Hoo in Kent and St Katharine's Dock, next to the Tower of London.

SOCIETIES
*The Cirdan Trust*, Chief Executive, Fulbridge Wharf, Maldon, Essex CM9 7LE.
*East Coast Sail Trust*, Arley Grange, Burnham Road, Latchingdon, Essex CM3 6EY. (Both this and the Cirdan Trust provide sailing and character-building cruises for young people.)
*Thames Barge Sailing Club*, c/o National Maritime Museum, Greenwich, London SE10 9NF. Website: www.bargeclub.org